FUEL FROM THE FENS

A PORTRAIT OF THE FENLAND TURF INDUSTRY IN CAMBRIDGESHIRE

ANTHONY DAY

S.B. Publications

By the same author:
Turf Village (1983)
Wicken: A Fen Village in Old Photographs (1990)
Fen and Marshland Villages (1993)
But For Such Men as These (1994)
Farming in the Fens (1995)
Wicken: A Second Selection of Old Photographs (1996)
Times of Flood (1997)

First published in 1999 by S.B. Publications
19 Grove Road, Seaford, East Sussex BN25 1TP

ISBN: 1 85770 190 9

Printed and bound by
MFP Design and Print,
Longford Trading Estate,
Thomas Street, Stretford,
Manchester M32 0JT

CONTENTS

Front cover: The Victorian painter of the fens, Robert Farren of Cambridge, responded to the languorous romanticism of his age in this study of turf workers near Wicken, an etching of 1882. While two ladies add to the stack with pre-Raphaelite elegance there would hardly be another in repose and an idle man flagrantly disregarding the piecework wages in force at the time. It was just that the artist would not be denied his compositional needs.

Back cover: This is Robert Farren who specialised in views of the fens in the second half of the nineteenth century. He missed little of obvious pictorial appeal, including its drainage mills, its wildlife, its rivers, riverside pubs and landworkers applying themselves in the spirit of Millet. He was a skilled etcher whose topographical works were published in huge volumes. He was in competition with photographers at that time, one of them being his brother, but he preceded them with his studies.

(Cambridgeshire Collection)

ACKNOWLEDGEMENTS

I thank Birmingham Library Services for allowing me to use the P.J. Deakin photographs in their collection, Mr T.A. Rowell for the aerial view and the Cambridge Folk Museum for their cooperation. I could not have done without the reminiscences, set down several years ago, of the late Henry and Mary Barnes, the late Reggie Butcher, the late Walter Redit, the late Gilbert Robinson and, of course, the late Bert Bailey. And, as always, I am grateful for the willing help given by Chris Jakes and his staff at the Cambridgeshire Collection and the welcome given by Steve Benz.

INTRODUCTION

Created by a colossal interglacial tide sweeping inland and carrying all before it, the fens of East Anglia between Cambridge, Peterborough, Lincoln and The Wash remained for centuries seemingly uninhabitable. The first settlers on the silt islands that we know as towns and villages soon learned to sustain themselves on fish, wildfowl and produce from the waters below. They used the reeds, sedge and willows for their dwellings while relying on skins, fleeces and feathers for their bodily protection. But in this region where trees could never thrive in significant numbers they had little else to burn for their winter comfort but cattle dung and that in very limited supply. That is, until the discovery of a fuel below the waters, come upon by chance, perhaps, when the dried residue dug from a channel refused to flare when set alight but instead smouldered to give off a consistent heat.

Thus began an industry long ago, perhaps before the Romans arrived, although it was not in place sufficiently to merit inclusion in the Domesday Book. Not long after, however, life became a lot warmer for the hardy settlers in waterlogged winter fenland as the turf-digging industry burgeoned. From the thirteenth century claims and disputes about turbaries, as the turf-diggings were called, were frequent and widespread, sometimes relating to common turbaries which came to be as essential to the region as common pastures, the disputes often relating to lords of the manor choosing to exert restrictions or exact dues within their claimed boundaries.

This product of decayed vegetation, found also in huge quantities abroad and composed principally of reeds, rushes, sedge and moss, truly brought civilisation to the fens by providing a steady source of income, even a relatively high standard of living, for its workers compared with other labouring opportunities. The industry continued well into the twentieth century until conceding at last to the effects of fen drainage and reducing demand through the availability of coal via the railways, coal offering double the heat of turf of the same weight. Thus the trade exhausted itself before it became undesirable to undertake such work where the money was available but hard-earned.

Perforce I confine myself here to the turbaries between the Cambridgeshire villages of Wicken, Burwell, Reach and Swaffham Prior simply because they outlasted all others and remained in place long enough to attract the photographers wanting to preserve images of a dying industry. These were ideal turf villages with their ancient lodes for transportation and ample resources of peat until the last pit was abandoned in Swaffham Fen soon after the outbreak of the second world war. The last digger there and anywhere was Bert Bailey (1887-1982), my uncle, who joined his father John (1858-1936) in the trade at the age of twelve in 1899. Soon after the closure came the old turf areas of Burwell and Swaffham Fen went under the plough for the war effort.

Peat was ever turf when dug for fuel. It was there warming the winter classrooms of Wickens school into the nineteen-thirties, but in those carpetless, curtainless spaces we welcomed the extra warmth of coal when it came while missing the herbal fumes of the smouldering turf gradually reducing to a creamy ash from which the new fire could be easily revived in the morning. Yes, the lady teacher did her best, for her protection alone, to tarnish the air with her dousings of disinfectant, but it gave her useful exercise to slip from her stool at intervals to lay another turf on the glowing stack, then to gesture the residue from her elegant fingers. She could leave coal until the intervals.

Beneath the essential upper layer of peat in the fens, which could be as much as thirty feet, were layers of silt sandwiching earlier peat, now no better than mud, betraying the formations of the area over many centuries. Inevitably the digging of turf contributed to the lowering of the land, but in the early waterlogged days the peat restored itself for such a relatively sparse population incapable of over-production. After the seventeenth century drainage became effective the level began to sink through erosion and thus began the race against time for the turf industry and, eventually, for the fens themselves.

THE OLD FEN, WICKEN

The fame of Wicken Fen as a nature reserve maintaining the character of primeval fenland has stood for well over a hundred years. Its continued existence as such was due to the determination of men from Wicken and surrounding villages to oppose the scheme for draining the fens in the reign of Charles I. These men like their forebears for hundreds of years depended on the produce of the fen and they wanted their lives to remain the same. With support from local dignitaries, including a Justice of the Peace whose sympathies precluded prosecuting any rebel, they won their battle to retain what other fenmen were to lose, while knowing that the drainage system would gradually encroach on the quality of their lives. Their victory, achieved with mob threats, stones and pitchforks, not to mention spades and shovels to refill dykes, is followed today by a continuous effort to retain the essential character of the fen for naturalists and thousands of visitors a year. This engraving of the fen in 1878 was taken from a drawing by E.L. Wheeler. The whole of this fen was once dug for turf, but its harvest thereafter was sedge, taken from privately owned strips until the National Trust took over.

(Cambridgeshire Collection)

THE FEN ON FIRE

Generally waterlogged in winter, with scope for skating about its fringes, Wicken Fen could become inflammably dry in summer. Fire had threatened it before, but the inferno of August 15th 1929, which I well remember, brought its sedge, scrub and reeds to the ground. A carelessly cast cigarette was the likely cause. The arrival of fire engines to alert the whole village could do nothing to halt the fire which burned out to the water barriers. The firemen could but stand by the thatched cottages near the fen to douse any flying spark. Of these local men I recognise three from their silhouetted heads, being, left, Dick Bailey and Jack Nixon and at the right, Harold Crow. One year on the fen was alive and green again, its wildlife returned, the old turf trenches once more revealed.

(Author's Collection)

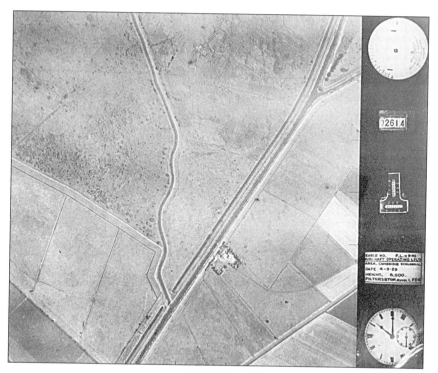

FROM THE AIR

Once the sedge-cutting was brought to an end by the National Trust the scrub began to push through the peat. At first the naturalists were intrigued to see what grew there, but before they could worry about it taking over the fire took the bushes away. It became an ideal moment for photographing the fen from the air to record its ancient markings. This view, taken at a quarter-past-one on 4th September 1929, shows Wicken Sedge Fen at the top, left, behind Wicken Lode, the old turf trenches just visible. On the right of the lode is Lapwing, Adventurers' Fen, spreading into Burwell Fen, the site of the turbaries covered by this book. Cutting across the picture is Commissioners' Drain, running alongside Burwell Lode, beyond which is South Adventurer's Fen, which was dug intensively for turf.

(Author's Collection)

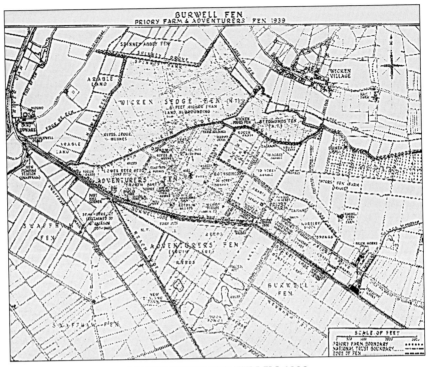

ADVENTURERS' FEN IN 1939

Long abandoned by the turf diggers, the north and south parts of Adventurer's Fen, the settings for this book, appeared like this at the outbreak of the second world war. Later the War Agricultural Committee decided upon reclamation of the land for food production at that time of national need and Mr Alan Bloom, living at Priory Farm, was made responsible for the job. A film was made of the enterprise, now in the East Anglian Film Archive.

(Faber and Faber)

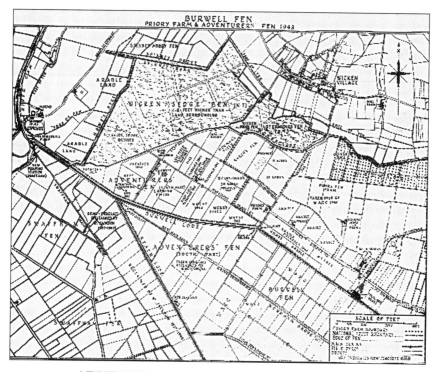

ADVENTURERS' FEN UNDER THE PLOUGH

The cost of reclaiming this landscape of bogs created by turf digging and left thereafter to grow wild was enormous, but the rich peatland gave forth enormous crops to compensate, proportioned as shown here. After the war the north or Wicken side of Burwell Lode was left to revert to the wild again and a mere was dug there for the National Trust in the 1950s. Bloom's men had encountered huge bog-oaks to impede their progress and many more have surfaced since, both from the mere and from the land on the south side which has remained under the plough. All the land on the north side is now in the hands of the National Trust.

(Faber and Faber)

BOG OAKS

There were solid obstructions in the turf bogs that remained so to the ploughs later. These were - and are - bog oaks, felled as before an avalanche during the formation of the fens and preserved hard by the peat. If not all oaks, the ones lying a few feet down after prolonged erosion of the peat most certainly are and are sometimes forty feet long in the trunk and weighing as much as eight tons. They are hugely difficult to shift and are as black as coal. Much time was spent removing them by Alan Bloom's men after the last turf diggers had bypassed them. They had to be sawn into sections and dragged by horses and tractors to a new resting place where they could rot slowly, but Bloom resorted to blowing them up. Cutting them to pieces for fuel while there was turf at hand was never on. The wood smouldered much like turf leaving a pinkish ash but fenmen seldom burnt it. These huge trunks testify to the sudden formation of the fens by pointing in the same direction. What a sight and sound that must have been if there was any human there to witness it. The oak above was uncovered near Soham Mere on the north side of Wicken during the second world war.

(M.R. Barton)

WICKEN

Wicken is known widely for its fen, but the village has its separate historical importance, not only for uprisings against drainage but as the birthplace of Isaac Barrow, Bishop of Sodor and Man, and the resting place of Henry Cromwell, sturdiest of the Protector's sons who retired here after resolute service in his father's cause in Ireland. Wicken also happens to be the archetypal turf village with its ancient waterways, known as lodes, for transportation, where the commodity was replaced but gradually as a fuel during the 1920s and where the industry ended in 1939.

This is the village pond c.1910, as instantly recognisable today. Two of the far cottages have gone and a new one filled the space second from the left in 1913, while that on the right was replaced by a dignified replica in the 1960s. The mill stands as proudly today, restored by enthusiasts to function in the near future.

(Author's Collection)

LODE LANE

The road from the north end of Wicken down to the fen is Lode Lane, at the foot of which lived no fewer than eleven families at the time of this photograph, c.1900, and long after that. Many of them, including the women and boys left school, depended on the turf industry for a living, including Billy 'Puddn' Bailey, fifth from the left, and Fred 'Stubby' Bailey, sixth from the left, whose children stand at the front with his wife, Clara, by the gate at the right.

(E.S. Aspland)

LODE LANE COTTAGES

Some ten years on this view captures some of the Lode cottages in this hamlet on its own. Those on the immediate left, home of turf-digger John Butcher, and the right, home of George his brother, George's son Robert, then Robert's widow, Alice and their son Reg, remain, the latter now a show cottage having been restored using the local reeds and sedge to show the authentic accommodation used by the locals long ago, and the way they kept their gardens. Sadly the other cottages, so much older and using the local materials including turves for insulation, were demolished as they were acquired by the National Trust since there were no funds to restore them. The coming and going of the turf hawkers with ponies and carts is clearly marked on the road.

(Author's Collection)

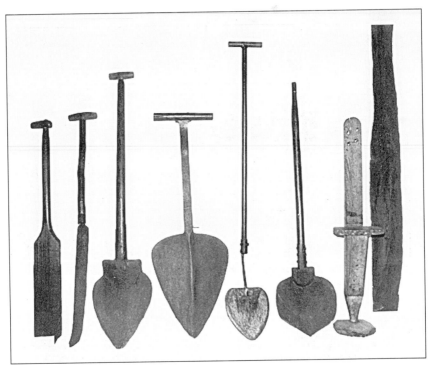

THE TURF DIGGER'S TOOLS

These are the basic tools used by the turf diggers from early times to the invention of the becket, a spade like a cricket bat with a right-angled flange, added to score two cuts at a thrust (left). Following, left to right, are a turf knife, used to cut alongside the intended trench, or pit as they were always called, then four moor spades, or sharp-shovels, the tool for all purposes before the becket was used but retained for part of the job thereafter. With water accumulating in the trench, as it often did, the digger might stand on stilts, such as seen on the right, but more often than not he would wear leather thigh boots well greased for insulation. Only during the late stages of the industry were rubber Wellingtons introduced.

(Nick Carter (Courtesy of the Cambridge County Folk Museum))

THE PROCEDURE

In Wicken the season for turf digging began in the first week in March and ended in the last week in August. It is June 1892 here in North Adventurers' Fen, a site dug extensively for turf for many years. The digger demonstrating for the cameras is John 'Mad Jack' Darnell (1832-1906) of Soham who walked some four miles to these pits every weekday and got home very late while beer was accessible to him at the 'Black Horse' at the head of Lode Lane. He was never late in the morning and his intake never altered the precision of his workmanship, a characteristic of every turf digger. The diggers started each working day at 6am and finished at 3pm,well before the mosquitoes swarmed in the evening air. Jack is digging on Harrison's land where the pits were always dug in line with Burwell Lode. At Lapwing, nearer Wicken Lode, owned by Wicken merchant Josiah Owers, the pits were always directed away from Burwell Lode. John's dress is like that of any landworker of the day apart from the net over his cap which he might dip in the water to cool his head, or thread with sprigs to ward off the flies, or use to cover his mouth from the morning mists that most men feared.

(P.J. Deakin; Birmingham Library Services)

MAKING THE PIT

John had pegged a long line to ensure a straight pit before clearing the surface vegetation down to about fifteen inches using his heart-shaped moor spade, which would then be used to shave the exposed peat to a flat surface, the term for this being to 'crumb-up'. More vegetation would be shaven from the side of the pit where the turves were to be placed. The cutlass-like turf knife would then be used to cut alongside the pit and the digger was ready to take out his harvest. He would be working backwards and very soon into his mechanical action pushing the becket into the soft turf, lifting out each sod or hassock, as they were sometimes called, and building a neat wall beside him three turves high with a broken row on top. Each saturated turf would then weigh about six to seven pounds using the Wicken becket, the handle of which was adjustable and held by nothing better than a piece of string.

(P.J. Deakin; Birmingham Library Services)

12

SHAPING THE TURVES

Call this an act for the camera since it was unlikely such a skilled worker as John Darnell would have to spend much time trimming his already trim turves. We saw him digging at a slant, but some diggers prided themselves on digging straight down. In this district the becket was first used in Isleham Fen in the 1850s. This was about fourteen inches long in the blade and three inches wide and the turves from it were generally sold by the hundred since selling by weight had suffered abuse through water being splashed on the turves before distribution. For large consignments to Cambridge, Wisbech and King's Lynn, however, it was necessary to sell by weight for loading onto barges.

Wicken's turf owners sooner decided to enlarge their becket to eighteen inches by four-and-a-half inches to speed up production, but not to give added measure for the Isleham price. They reduced their hundred to sixty yet still termed it a hundred, to which the hawkers soon became used while any newcomer felt cheated. The local blacksmiths made the beckets, using red willow for the handle. The flange was about an inch shorter that the width of the blade and with the peat being soft they needed little whetting. In the distance here the tall chimneys of the two Upware pumping stations can be seen, both essential to the drainage of this level.

(P.J. Deakin; Birmingham Library Services)

13

A PROUD MAN'S PERSPECTIVE

Here at Harrison's land we see the perfect order favoured by dedicated turf men. Slide-rule precision was in their nature, just as was the straight furrow to the born ploughman. The arms did all the digging and the pits would be dug one spit down and four across all the way across the allotted field, and if the decision after that was to continue another spit down this would always be only three turves wide. A wide area would be dug before the field was abandoned but there would be ample space between the pits for the barrowing. The cleared vegetation would be spaded into the pits and the field would be left to grow wild and flood for many years. Any return to it for turf would be for that already formed at the previous dig since new formations took more than a lifetime under suitable wet conditions. Subsequent farming along with erosion has shifted evidence of the old pits, but in St Edmunds Fen, Wicken, they lay waterlogged in winter to this day, meaning that peat has continued to form there. The foreground barrow here holds 'bits', the term for misshapen turves which were sold cheaply. In the background is Eustace Ball's mill, draining pits on the other side of Burwell Lode. In fierce winds its bearings once heated up and burned the mill down.

(P.J. Deakin; Birmingham Library Services)

LAPWING

The last three Wicken turf merchants were Mark Bailey, a farmer, Bill Norman, farmer, shopkeeper, coal merchant and postmaster, and Josiah Owers, come in from Birmingham as the village carpenter but wanting like the others to add to his income. Josiah's turf fields were at Lapwing, the triangle of land where Wicken Lode joins Burwell Lode. Remarkably a family had once set up home in the middle of Lapwing, but how they kept dry in winter remains a mystery. Their residence was known as Lapwing Hall to keep company with Ragamore Castle, a crude hut dwelling by Monks' Lode. A field nearer Burwell was Harrison's land with his home nearby and equally vulnerable to the conditions. Here we see fifteen-year-old Robert Butcher of Wicken loading the barrow with bits in 1892 on Josiah's land, the pit beside him typically waterlogged. Josiah would be lucky to see his men digging before April but to persuade them to produce early he promised them a sausage supper should they get a boatload of turf home and dry by Wicken Feast, May 13th. That turf would not be sold until the autumn since it needed six months from digging to burning.

(P.J. Deakin; Birmingham Library Services)

DRAINAGE

While the fens were above mean tide level it was necessary to cut channels to take off the surface water, but once erosion began to bring the level down pumps had to be installed to lift the water into those channels. The first were horse-powered, followed by windmills such as persisted to the end of the turf-digging era. These, known as 'outliers' were used to drain the turbaries and this is Josiah Owers' mill at Lapwing by Commissioners' Drain, a skeleton mill not only for economical reasons but to resist the powerful winds used to drain the site before the digging began. The sails then could get up such speed that the water was spun nearly as high by the scoopwheels. The bearings then took the strain and could catch fire, as Eustace Ball discovered to his cost.

(Cambridgeshire Collection)

THE DIGGERS' SHELTER

If turf digging was not exactly heavy work it demanded great energy and concentration, as did the associative jobs of dressing, or re-stacking the turves by the pit leaving gaps to hasten the drying, and barrowing to the stacks or boats, which had to be done for the piecework wages. In summer the men were sweltering in their pits, their thirsts insatiable, the flies maddening, the need for rest, shade and refreshment acute. For Bert Bailey, who was taught his trade as well as his liking for beer by John Darnell, these associated jobs brought him five shillings per thousand turves in his younger days. He and his father, aiming at a record, once dug ten thousand turves in a day, while the dressing was done at the rate of two to three thousand an hour! They took advantage of such crude shelters as this at Lapwing c.1910 where they could brew up, on a turf fire, their popular coffee 'messes', which included broken bread and sugar. Thirsts often had to be slaked from the lodes, which ran pure then. Left to right here are John Butcher with his dog Spot, Jabez Bell and at the right Fred 'Stubby' Bailey, all of Wicken, with Eli Mansfield of Burwell, builder of turf boats.

(Author's Collection)

THE LONER

Fred 'Stubby' Bailey, sitting here by the same shelter, and his wife Clara produced a big family, but he liked nothing better than to work in solitude. He spent his working life in the turf trade but his four sons preferred, or were directed to, the farming life. At this time before the first world war some three hundred men and boys, plus a few women, were still engaged in the turf industry between the villages of Wicken, Burwell and Reach, but after that war the numbers declined rapidly. Their turves were not only used for burning. Crude dwellings were once made of them bound in withers with roofs of osiers and reeds. The outer walls would receive a facing of clay to keep the weather out. A cottage pulled down in Lode Lane, Wicken some forty years ago revealed a layer of turves under the roof, each harder than bark. The fumes from smouldering turves were considered benign enough to assist the breathing of hospital patients and employers advertising for domestic servants would mention their turf fires to attract them. Fifteen turves propped against one another were considered enough to heat a cottage baking oven while the village bakers needed far more. Blacksmiths favoured turf fires, sometimes mixed with wood, for heating their iron tyres for tumbril wheels. Old, hardened turves were sometimes laid down for land drains, but the fen peat holds little value for gardeners.

(Author's Collection)

LOADING THE BOATS

This is Robert Butcher (1877-1922) loading turves on the boat on Wicken Lode c.1908. The barrows were well-designed to balance the loads and were six feet long from the extremes of the wheel and handles which were just over two feet apart. A few examples still remain in Wicken. A man would carry two hundred turves at a time on these open barrows but a boy, always with hazards ahead and for his own safety, would take only a hundred.

Digging rights were sold by the owners of the land, or the owners, as in the case of the last three Wicken merchants, employed men to work for them. These merchants were uncanny in being able to judge the quality of turf below from the vegetation growing on top. Prices of fifty to eighty pounds an acre have been recorded for a prolonged deep dig, but Bert Bailey insisted his owner employer required turf to the value of twenty-two pounds an acre digging one spit deep.

(Author's Collection)

THE BALANCING ACT

Boys were compelled to accustom themselves to this balancing act and it took time. To steel them in this enterprise the turf men gave them to understand that should they topple into the drain, barrow, turves and all, they would be compelled to buy a gallon of beer for their workmates. It happened quite often and caused fun more than anger. Bert Bailey well remembered paying his due and vowing to hold on to his hard-earned money thereafter. This is Commissioners' Drain running alongside Burwell Lode. It was also known during its last days of use as Jethro's Drain after Jethro Granfield of Wicken, the superintendent of the Burwell Engine at Upware at that time. Two spars three inches thick and six inches wide were bolted together, leaving a gap between to allow for swelling, to help guide the barrow wheel and to ensure a steady, predictable bounce for the crossings. The planks could bend alarmingly under the weight of a heavy man with a full barrow. Spiked boots were useful when the planks were wet and slippery. On the soft fen side a grooved trough was pushed to the bottom of the drain as here, ensuring a safe descent before the uphill climb. Then came the steeper climb up the lode bank to the boat, assisted sometimes by trestles and planks.

(Scott and Wilkinson)

THE LOADED BOATS

It is June 1892 and the river banks at this time were worn bare and hard and were much used for journeys on cycles between the villages. The wear and tear, however, was made by the haling ponies or donkeys. These are Josiah Owers' boats on Burwell Lode ready to move off from Lapwing to Wicken. At the bow is Fred Stubby with Robert Butcher by the donkey. The loading had been done as neatly as any part of the operation, the turves inclining inwards for safety. Traditionally the loads consisted of eleven thousand turves aboard a gang of three small boats but the men here have gauged the load with regard for the deepest channel to be navigated, allowing spare freeboard for sinking lower. Water levels were high at this time and the men were experienced in their routes. Arriving at the Cockup Bridge spanning Wicken Lode, the donkey would be unhitched and the boats poled under before the donkey was reattached for the voyage home.

(P.J. Deakin; Birmingham Library Services)

THE HALING DONKEY

The donkey was preferred to the pony for haling turf boats. Once under way this little animal could comfortably pull those traditional three laden boats and their natural stubbornness could be an advantage, ensuring a steady pace even when pointing homewards at the end of the working day which kept down the head of water. A hungry homeward-bound pony was hard to restrain. The size of the donkey held another advantage. Coming to the junction of Monks' Lode near Wicken they could easily be taken aboard to be reconnected on the other side. This view of the haling donkey at work shows Bill Barnes, the first keeper of Wicken Fen, in charge and probably conveying a boatload of sedge.

(Author's Collection)

THE PRIORY COCKUP BRIDGE

This view of c.1900 shows the static version of the original Cockup Bridge over Burwell Lode near Priory Farm. That original had a moveable platform, held up by weights for masted river traffic, coming down easily for road traffic and rising up behind them. The replacements were high but masts had to be lowered to get under them. Made of wood, they were frequently repaired until this one was replaced by a concrete structure in the 1960s with the loss of picturesque charm and the reassuring tang of creosote.

(Cambridgeshire Collection)

WICKEN LODE COCKUP BRIDGE

Crossing Wicken Lode at the junction of Burwell Lode, this replacement bridge managed to hold together until its picturesqueness was seen as a virtue in itself, ensuring a new facsimile in 1996. This is where the turf boats turned off for Wicken for the winding voyage home. These bridges were favoured for picnics and today they make good viewing platforms over the fens that have sunk dramatically from the original level. While the turf digging continued the bridges served another purpose as we shall see.

(Cambridgeshire Collection)

NORMAN'S BRIDGE

This, in 1929, is the crude crossing built for Bill Norman to save transporting his donkey or pony over Monks' Lode in the boat, but if John and Bert Bailey transported themselves home in an empty boat, as they frequently did, they invariably led the donkey aboard to save walking with it some way up the bank and back again. It was simply quicker. The turf men loved their donkeys and ponies like pets and protected them at all times. Once it had retired with him, Bert Bailey nurtured his donkey to the end of its long life, then planted an oak tree over its grave. I rode that donkey as a boy - just once, which was enough for anybody!

(Cambridgeshire Collection; Reid)

THE ARRIVAL

Fluctuating prices were always part of the turf-digging industry, these often influenced by national crises and consequent opportunism. During the Napoleonic wars, for instance, prices were double those of fifty years later while the coal shortage during the first world war stimulated prices to as much as thirty shillings per thousand. Owners took advantage of the General Strike of 1926 to deliver turf in place of coal to the Cambridge Colleges. Estimated by weight, the price was only fifteen shillings a ton for the supplier in 1900. One hundred and seventy-six tons of turf were transported, mainly from Burwell and Wicken, to Cambridge alone in 1905 and it was still being taken there, if in declining quantities, after the first world war.

The boy above awaits space on the other side for unloading at the end of Wicken Lode. Eli Mansfield made the boats to suit the needs of each client. Each liked to show his trademark as a matter of pride. For Josiah Owers, Eli raised the bows more than most and painted them red while Mark Bailey chose a narrower boat painted all black.

(Author's Collection)

HOME FROM THE HARD DAY

Arriving from the pits in the 1890s is George Butcher, Robert's father who outlived him. His dog Billy here is no more the pet than his donkey, Reuben, which is to say they were equal companions. George lived in Lode Lane in the house built for him, the one now restored to its original character as an attraction for the many visitors to the fen. George also farmed later from Field Farm near Upware where Robert joined him after his mother had died. Robert, however, died within the year aged 45 and George with Alice, Robert's widow, and their son Reggie, returned to the paternal cottage where George died in 1936. The Butchers came from nearby Stretham, as it happened from a family of butchers.

THE TURF SHEDS

Wet weather delayed production and drying, windless wet weather brought flooding and high tides and river levels put the mills on hold and made matters worse, but the turf stacks grew each year to meet the all-the-year-round demand. These are the turf sheds below Lode Lane, Wicken in June 1892 belonging to the last three turf merchants. On the left nearest the village is the shed owned by Josiah Owers, a privilege costing him a five shillings-a-year mooring fee to the parish council, double that paid by bill Norman, whose shed, covered half with sedge and half corrugated iron, is in the middle, and Mark Bailey whose shed just appears on the right. Mark stands out on the left in a white shirt beside a cart that had just deposited stones for road resurfacing. These were collected by boys off farmland for the farmers who could pay a proportion of their rates with them. The boat on the left belongs to Josiah, the other two to Mark.

(P.J. Deakin; Birmingham Library Services)

STORAGE

Inside the sheds the turves were built on slats to keep the air circulating, but the constant demand ensured hefty stacks outside the sheds for most of the year. Huge stacks were left by the turf pits, taking the winter very well although persistent frost might crumble the outside turves which were left marked into thousands. Many were destined for voyages to the towns. Vestiges of those stacks would remain by the drain when the new season began, for supplies were always kept way ahead of demand. These two sheds are Mark Bailey's with the man himself standing left in the boat with his son, Lister Arthur but known as Arthur Mark, standing right. Ellen, Mrs George Butcher, who died aged seventy-six while George lived to be eighty-three, is the other figure taking a 'hand' of turf, meaning three turves at a time, the swiftest way of handling them for the hawkers. She, like other women in the lane, stood by to offer this service and to help unload the boats.

(E.S. Aspland)

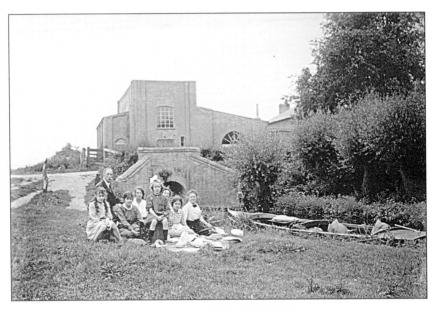

THE BURWELL ENGINE

Taking the water of Commissioners' Drain through to the River Cam was the Burwell Engine, seen here after its tall chimney had been felled following the change from coal to gas power. While taking the water from the turf pits it was also ensuring their demise. The engine ceased to function long ago and the drain is now no more than a shallow ditch. The shed as seen here has survived and at the present time is being adapted as an unusual private home. Here before the first world war the drain is navigable, but not for the loaded turf boats which used the lode out of the picture on the left passing through the sluice. The party are basking in an era of peace soon to come to an appalling end.

(Cambridgeshire Collection)

THE SWAFFHAM ENGINE

This Upware pumping station functions today but not in this building that was built in 1851 and pulled down in 1939. There had been a change from steam power to diesel in 1927, leaving this building on standby but virtually redundant. It replaced an earlier shed built in 1821. It served South Adventurer's Fen and Swaffham Fen but today also takes in the area once covered by the Burwell engine. The Stevens family controlled this great engine for many years. William, formerly of the Hundredfoot Engine near Little Downham and before that a blacksmith, was succeeded by his son Arthur who took retirement soon after the installation of the diesel engine. Upware was a closely knit community before the first world war and for some time after, built around its two pumping stations, two pubs and its shop-cum-post office.

(Rosa Stevens)

A TURF DIGGER'S FAMILY

The turf digger was always able to earn more money than the farm worker - and many of them, as here, needed it. David Bailey and his wife Mary of Wicken were photographed here in the 1890s at Hunstanton, probably while on a Methodist excursion. A turf digger, or cutter, as some liked to call them, clearly was able to keep his large family well fed and clothed while many farm workers' families of this size were in dire poverty. Left to right, the girls at the back are Nelly and Sarah, the boys in the middle James, Sidney and Ezra and at the front Louis, Arthur and Polly. Arthur emigrated to America. If there had been room for more turf diggers the vast majority of men would not have taken on the job.

(Author's Collection)

JOHN BUTCHER

George Butcher's brother John was a turf digger, seen here in the 1930s, a warm, likeable man who married twice. His second wife fostered three Barnados children, two brothers and a sister. John was one of many who also dug turves for his own use in the common turbaries within Poor's Fen and Poor's Piece, part of Wicken Sedge Fen. The men who dug there often chose larger beckets in the cause of quantity since the allotted time for digging there was limited. They were not allowed to begin digging before the third Monday in July and they were not allowed to hire assistants. They dug there haphazardly so that today Poor's Fen is a pot-holed morass covered with reeds and scrub. Household rubbish was thrown into many of the old pits. John Butcher hired land for his own commercial use where he was reputed to have used a smaller than usual becket to conserve supplies. At six inches wide, the blade used by George King in the common turbaries is the widest I have ever seen. There were many variations on the shape and size of the becket in other parts of the fens. In Coveney, near Ely, for instance, the original becket measured nine-and-a-half inches long by six-and-a-half inches wide and the squarer blocks from it found favour for a long time.

(Author's Collection)

THE BAILEYS

Bailey was the commonest name in Wicken until well after the second world war. Most of them descended from Richard Bailey and Margaret Haylock who were married in 1721. Huge families descended from them but the line is vanishing from the village today. This is Bert Bailey, last of the professional fen turf diggers, at the age of ninety-three, seen sitting outside the 'Maid's Head' in Wicken, his most frequently attended social club just yards from his home. He died two years later at ninety-five. His mother lived to a hundred, one of his sister's to almost a hundred-and-three. No man enjoyed the tavern life more without ever giving offence. The brewery owning the 'Maid's Head' honoured him with a free pint of beer every day during his last two years. He talked of his old trade many times on television, even singing a song on one programme. He was the first in Wicken to volunteer for service in the first world war from which he emerged unscathed.

(Richard Harvey)

DUMB FRIEND

Haling donkeys and ponies remained family pets, particularly where there were children in the family. They were well fed, fussed over and deeply mourned when they died, the donkeys generally at a ripe old age, like Reuben here, George Butcher's donkey held by George's son John who sadly died soon after at the age of fifteen. Nobby, the pony owned by Bill Barnes, once haled along the river routes, knew all the riverside pubs and was known to the landlords who gave him beer. He pulled barges of visitors from Wicken to Upware and is talked of today. Ponies were favoured by the hawkers who regularly picked up supplies from the turf sheds. The owners seldom hawked their own turves but John and Bert Bailey, when the industry was in decline and they had the time to spare, delivered turf around Wicken while Bill Barnes tried it as one of his many enterprises aiming to feed a family of twelve. The first professional hawker coming from Soham in the 1900s was Elizabeth Ann Martin who loaded her cart so full she had to ride on the step or walk. She was walking homeward on October 12th 1905 when for no reason that the one witness could explain the horse bolted and Mrs Martin fell under the wheel and was killed.

(E.S. Aspland)

FRED 'STUBBY'S' DONKEY

The donkeys had their leisure uses too, as here, so long as they were not tired. This is Fred Stubby's donkey, at ease on a Sunday, betrayed by the clothes the boys are wearing. They are Fred's boys Reg, astride and Cecil. Ben Rust took over from Mrs Martin as Soham's turf hawker and he was followed by Gilbert Robinson after the first world war when inflation and demand enabled him to make as much as ten pounds a week. I met this man during the last year of his life when he was too ill to elaborate about his life apart from telling me he fetched five loads of turf every two days from either Wicken or Burwell. An account book used by the first Mrs John Butcher records that Ben Rust payed eleven shillings and sixpence per thousand turves in 1915 but eighteen shillings in 1918. Leniency is shown to local people fetching their small quantities as they were needed.

(Author's Collection)

LEISURE ON SITE

Here where Wicken Lode begins John 'Bunyan' Bailey takes his rest in an empty turf boat while three children take advantage of a mooring. It is hardly a Sunday since there is washing on the line. Leisure was little more than rest in June 1992 and that was bliss enough for such hard-working men. The stack of sedge behind belongs to Robert Aspland who as the local storekeeper advertised his sedge for sale. In that capacity he was the last in a line that began in the village in the 1740s. His daughter Emma Sophia was a genius with a camera who took more photographs than have survived in the village.

(P.J. Deakin; Birmingham Library Services)

THE DIVING PLATFORM

The young, of course, needed more than rest for leisure. They became used to hard work and had plenty of energy left afterwards. Here in the 1920s they make use of the Priory Cockup Bridge as if it were made solely for the purpose. The lodes were not deep but they could accommodate a high dive and it was show-off time for all. The waters were pure then and the lodes were the bathing places for adults and children. For a young teenager Monks' Lode might reach above his middle but a lot of that was mud but here in Burwell Lode you would need to be a swimmer. This lode has now been taken out of the drainage system and is preserved for boating and fishing but the banks are no longer worn bare by the haling donkeys.

(Cambridgeshire Collection; Grainger)

ALL ABOARD FOR THE VOYAGE

This is a sedge boat out of commission for the day since it is August Bank Holiday 1931 and Bill Barnes is preparing a trip to Upware and the 'Five Miles from Anywhere - No Hurry' pub for a modest fare apiece. It was just one of his many cash-earning enterprises. Another when the rivers were frozen hard was to take out his wheelbarrow that happened to be fitted with a cycle wheel, skate with it to Cambridge, buy it full of oranges, skate through to the skating match at Earith ten miles away, sell out and come home rich. The river trips were much appreciated when travel was limited to bus rides, cycle rides and shanks' pony. The ripple of pure water was relaxing as Nobby the pony haled them along and Bill pumped out tunes from his accordion, but coming back towards evening the mosquitoes could set the passengers slapping their necks. Left to right, the girls at the front are Dorothy Barnes, Olive Canham and Florence Barber while the dark-hatted ladies are Mrs Bob Canham and Mrs Bill Barnes.

(Author's Collection)

NO WORK ON SUNDAY

Here by Reach Lode in Swaffham Fen in the 1920s all is still and the walkers have come down from the bank to the turf shelter to pose for the photographer. Cyril Bailey, whose father was born in Wicken, holds the shafts while his mother sits on the cart, left, with Dorothy Bailey of Wicken. The turves are the remains of a stack. It was near this site, by Hubberstead's Farm, that Bert Bailey completed his last dig in 1939. Thereafter he did what jobs came up, including land work and helping in the fen while the parish council used him at the school and as a grave digger. There was never a job to suppress his happy nature. Then the media caught up with him.

(Author's Collection)

DECLINE AND FALL

And so goodbye to the old trade and its relics as they were left to the whims of nature. Josiah Owers' pits were closed well before the era finally ended but his mill was soon crumbling to the elements. It gradually sank into the peat and looked like this in the mid-1920s. Josiah's two sons succeeded him in his carpentry and building trade until they married and left the village, their sheds being taken over by Bill Simpkin of Wicken a reliable craftsman in wood who sold to one more carpenter before the business folded.

(Cambridgeshire Collection)

MARSHALL'S MILL

The wooden drainage mills served a useful purpose well into the twentieth century but once the turf bogs were closed the mills were left to fall apart. This mill near Wicken Sedge Fen looks smartly maintained here in the early 1920s. The sweeps, or cloths will have to be attached to set it going and the top is manoeuvreable from the ground to catch the wind. While it once had a lot of work to do the problem in Wicken Fen today is that it stands much higher than the surrounding landscape so that water has to be dammed into it, even pumped into it, to maintain the old character.

(Cambridgeshire Collection)

GOING, GOING...

Some ten years on the discarded Marshall's Mill is falling apart, no longer needed to lift the water. Bill Barnes stands in front of it for no other reason than it adds human interest for the photographer. People paid far more attention to the mills when they began collapsing into the peat. There is no sign of this one today. It was the sad duty of Bill Barnes to see the era of these windpumps out.

(Author's Collection)

THE PLAYGROUND

The wind grew impatient with this one at New Zealand by Reach Lode in Swaffham Fen. Bert Bailey was still digging not far away in 1937 and it must have been sad to see this happening. The scoopwheel looks to be in sound order with Bill Hawes on top but the body looks a little more precarious under John Wilson, two boys from Wicken, with visitor, Phillip Treen. The size and intricacy of the scoopwheel is indicated here, designed to push water upwards and stay intact. At long last there was but one of these mills left relatively intact near Wicken and the story of it follows.

(M.R. Barton)

NORMAN'S MILL

Bill Norman abandoned his turf bogs well before he died in 1919, leaving his old mill to fall apart. Then during the second world war when both South and North Adventurers' Fen were reclaimed for agriculture his mill was restored as seen above, left, and set to work. After the war when the land was left to grow wild the mill began to fall apart again until in the late 1940s the War Agricultural Committee, as it had been, repaired the mill once more (right), although not for use. Gradually the mill deteriorated again, the last such mill standing in this area.

(Cambridgeshire Collection (left); Keith Hinde (right))

ONCE MORE IN DECLINE

This is Norman's Mill in the 1950s, once again left to deteriorate until coming under the gaze of Lord Fairhaven of Anglesey Abbey at Lode who laid plans to rebuild. He decided to have it dismantled piece by piece and to rebuild it for Wicken Sedge Fen. The problem was to find a millwright sufficiently experienced to do such a job when it was now out of fashion. Happily that man was discovered in Histon near Cambridge, a carpenter by trade and an ailing man, but ready and willing to take up this challenge.

(Author's Collection)

ISON'S MILL

This is the man who rebuilt Norman's mill to full working order in 1956. He was C.J. Ison to whom the mill is dedicated who restored or rebuilt the parts in his workshops and assembled them on site. These following eight pictures tell the story more clearly than words. On the left are the original centres of the scoopwheels and the driving wheel. Mr Ison, of average height, stands to demonstrate the scale of the wheels. On the right he begins an entirely new body for the mill.

(E.D. Nisbet)

THE SCOOPWHEEL AND CAP

With little or no experience of the job Mr Ison has built new scoops for the old wheel with some help from a craftsmen in metal while on the right he has completed the frame for the new cap which also shows the bearing block for the sails shaft and the metal band and lever of the handbrake that could be applied to the sails shaft.

(E.D. Nisbet)

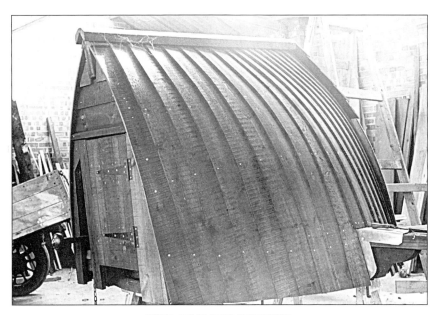

THE CAP COMPLETED

Admirably crafted and made to last, the cap is complete and ready for transportation to Wicken, the first and last for hundreds of years. You can sense the man's pride in his achievement, the born carpenter's love of wood and precision.

(E.D. Nisbet)

COMPLETION

In its place the cap looks small as the mill is put together in Wicken Fen. Mr Ison's two apprentices here are Leonard Froment and Bob Welford who are happy to do the climbing for him. The concrete base is an innovation, but this mill has to stay as a showpiece which is what the fen has become today. Its conservation has a lot to do with inactivity, but it functions for a true purpose when necessary. On the right the job is almost complete, the sweeps attached to catch the wind and away we go.

(E.D. Nisbet)

SILENCE ACROSS THE OLD TURF PITS

The girl was one of the party in the picture on page 29, stretching her legs carrying her butterfly net. Beyond her the landscape has long since grown green over the old turf bogs. In the distance Lapwing remains as silent as any landscape in England, a grazing area in part from the Wicken Cockup Bridge and reedbeds beyond which are harvested for thatching still.

(Cambridgeshire Collection)

THE LODE REACH. No. 306

REACH LODE

This is a very ancient waterway, possibly Roman, there today for the fishermen and those wanting peace. It is generally as quiet today as it is here around 1910 when it was used for deliveries of turf to the tiny village at the end of the Devil's Dyke. The fisherman here is after food, not sport, the guiding motive today. Round the bend here it arrives at The Hythe where the scene remains much the same. Reach people were buying turves right up to the second world war.

(Cambridgeshire Collection)

REACH

The road to the right leads down to The Hythe, while on the left here in the 1920s we have the 'Black Swan' and on the right the village shop and post office, both of which are no more. Here too we see motor transport gradually overtaking the horsedrawn carts, a meeting that much exercised the photographers at that time. The central green of this little village replaced the end of the Devil's Dyke after it had been levelled to make the two parts of the village one, one half having been in Burwell parish and the other half in Swaffham Prior. Turf fires were burning here at this time supplied by the bogs in Swaffham Fen, Wicken or Burwell, the local dab hand at the job being Seth Badcock, whom I knew later as an ace darts player.

(Cambridgeshire Collection)

53

REACH FROM THE DEVIL'S DYKE

The end of the dyke here affords a good view of the village that goes down to the fen. The dyke continues seven miles to Wooditton near Newmarket. Originally an ancient rampart, it is today a marvellous walk, a vantage point all the way. The Iceni probably constructed it while the Saxons used it as their boundary between Mercia and East Anglia. Reach was once an inland port and its annual fair, instituted by King John, continues today with local enterprises substituting for the travelling amusements. Far fewer natives live here than before but it has changed little in appearance for many years. We are looking at it here in the 1930s.

(Cambridgeshire Collection)

Fall Street, Soham.

SOHAM

The fen-edge villages of Wicken, Isleham, Burwell and Soham were ideally sited for the turf industry, with secure access from the high ground and placid waterways into the fen. Soham was ever more town than village, indisputably so today in having almost doubled its population since the time of this photograph, pre-first world war. It absorbed huge supplies of Wicken and Burwell turf to the very end of the era when a Soham man, Arthur Bradley, had become the last Wicken turf supplier, hiring the last bogs dug by Bert Bailey. As a coal merchant he thus bridged the eras of turf and coal, less for his own sake than for his cousin Bert.

(Cambridgeshire Collection)

FORDHAM

About four miles from Wicken and more closely attached to Soham, Fordham was very much on the delivery rounds of the turf hawkers at the time of this view of Market Street, c.1910. It became a village of horticultural nurseries and remains so today. The low land towards Isleham is Fordham Moor but the village had no immediate access to turf bogs and took further supplies of turf from Isleham.

(Cambridgeshire Collection; Gillson)

ARRIVING AT BURWELL

Uprisings over land set aside for the poor being sold to settle arrears of taxes occurred in Burwell in 1851, necessitating the attendance of the Metropolitan Police and the military to settle matters. It was resolved by a munificent parson who bought the land and gave it back to the parish. Among the rebels were turf men who having earned big money during the digging season had been spending it lavishly on drink when idle. The undulating site of Burwell Castle, now with no visible remains and a public amenity, belonged to King Stephen. Geoffrey de Mandeville, a pillager who had been a thorn in the side of two sovereigns, attacked this fort and was killed by an arrow from it. His corpse was excommunicated by the pope, was carried to the Temple in London and kept unburied there for years until the pope was satisfied that Mandeville's sons had made reparations for their father's sins. A spring on the site of the castle or fort was one of the sources of Burwell Lode, the other being The Weirs at the far end of the village.

(Cambridgeshire Collection; Gillson)

BURWELL

Beginning a mile from Swaffham Prior, another fen-edge village, the long winding street that is visible Burwell to the traveller passing through ends on fen level. The road bearing left to it is The Causeway, the one turning right is to Fordham. Burwell has doubled in size and population in recent years but the housing developments are hidden away from this main thoroughfare which once boasted six places of worship along its route. Its fifteenth century church is one of the finest in the county and while its Primitive Wesleyan and Congregational chapels have gone as such the Wesleyan and Baptist remain. Fredereck Gillson set up his photographic business here in the early 1900s and his small cottage remains. He liked nothing better than to run off a set of street views for sale and we are much indebted to him. After he left for Ipswich his successors were W. and D. Grainger. Most of the houses seen here remain.

(Cambridgeshire Collection; Gillson)

NORTH STREET

Having veered left at what was the King William IV pub into The Causeway we are nearing fen level in North Street which continues into The Broads, which so long ago was a vast lake, and The Weirs. Turning left before that is Factory Road leading into Little Fen Road and Priory Road, these elevated from droves after the second world war. Halfway along to Priory Farm, now out of commission, the factory was set up originally to process coprolite then to manufacture artificial fertilizers. On the other side of the drove was built a brick factory to utilise the deep resources of clay at hand which supplied the factory until its demise in the 1970s. In this photograph the high building on the right is the supplementary church of England, now closed as such. The pump, of course, has long since gone from this scene of c.1905.

(Cambridgeshire Collection; Gillson)

Burwell, Turf Series, No. 5.

THE BURWELL TURBARIES

We are in South Adventurers' Fen, with planks in the foreground where the surface is soft, giving passage to carts and barrows. These stacks of turf are distant from the waterway because they will be transported into Burwell by cart. This side of Adventurers' Fen was dug deeply in its last phase, in some places five spits down. When the site was abandoned for turf it became a pooled paradise for waterbirds and many other forms of wildlife. Eric Ennion, the Burwell doctor and naturalist, also, however, an enthusiastic hunter, wrote a book about his pleasure ground of Adventurers' Fen at this time. Then during the wartime reclamation, Alan Bloom wrote a book about that. He came across Ennion's hides and while sympathising with his point of view dedicated himself to doing his own job well for the exigencies of his time. It was amazing how much rich peat remained for his purpose. In this view we are in the 1920s.

(Cambridgeshire Collection)

THE DURRANTS

Hawkers, of course, liked to keep their own supplies of turf, building stacks in their yards when the demand was low and accessibility to the digging sites was easy. This scene is from the early 1900s in Burwell where the hawkers, Mr and Mrs Durrant appear more suitably dressed for the camera than the work in hand which is not the unloading of the barrow but loading it with a hundred turves for a nearby customer. The turf barrow was indispensable. Happy in their work here or pleased to be photographed, the couple eventually, when the turf trade fell away, became coal merchants, fetching their supplies from the station to their business premises in North Street.

THE DOE FAMILY OF BURWELL

The father owned a saddler's shop in Burwell while filling the roles of town crier and bill poster. Mrs Doe sold sweets and toys which she displayed on a stall for the village feast at Whitsun. This is their all-purpose cart outside Gillson's photographic premises c.1903, with the couple's son Arthur leaning for his portrait. Arthur, who became known as Mate or Matey, applied himself to various jobs of his own making, one of them. to the delectation of every surrounding village within easy reach of his pony and canopied cart, much like the one here, was the supplying of ice cream This business was ousted by the advent of Walls ice cream carried in tricycle carts in the early 1930s. But Matey, if gravely missed by the refined palates of the time, had other enterprises to contain and feed him, including the hawking of turf round Burwell. He was to have no successor to his various jobs since his son was killed in the second world war.

(Cambridgeshire Collection; Gillson)

THE TURF HAWKER

Years on, after stand-pipes had been installed in Burwell and long after he had made his last delivery of turf, Matey Doe puts his old hawker's cart on show, complete with the donkey that had served him for years and was threatening to outlive him. Such adaptable men as Matey were a feature of village life between the wars and earlier. When the supplies were local, as with turf, there was no need for more up-to-date transport. Such self-sufficient villages are a thing of the past. Long without the native fuel, any small fenland village is lucky to have a shop and post office, a school, or any inducement for a child to feel rooted in village life. And none will ever taste Matey Doe's exquisite ice cream!

(Cambridgeshire Collection; Grainger)

A STALWART OF SWAFFHAM FEN

In Swaffham Fen beyond Reach Lode this digger shows his expertness at the job. His turves are perfect where conditions above ground are summer dry and the digging has been preceded by mowing. That is no sown crop in the background but wild growth that would no longer be given time to rot down into new peat. I doubt if this man had given much thought to that where the turf had been dug for over seven hundred years without diminution of supply. But this is the 1920s and times are changing rapidly. The beard conceals his age but turf digging was probably his last occupation.

SWAFFHAM FEN DIGGERS

The monotony of turf digging and dressing can only now be imagined. It was close to assembly line work, keeping to a mechanical rhythm for the sake of the product and production. The diggers were seldom but deep drinkers, but many of them during the day liked to limit their intake of drink to keep their sweat down. Many landworkers kept to that rule during the long days of harvest, with the certainty of making up for it in the cool of evening. Nevertheless dehydration had to be offset and the liquid intake was more often cold tea or water. I doubt if these Swaffham Fen diggers in the 1920s have anything stronger in their hands - unless the photographer has brought it to them to break their daytime pledge. Good rest periods were essential, to straighten the back, break the enforced concentration and to exchange views.

(Cambridgeshire Collection; Grainger)

WET CONDITIONS

It is early in the turf season, the site still wintry, the conditions here in Swaffham Fen very wet underfoot for the digger who, nevertheless, feels unprecedentedly secure in his modern Wellington boots. Those old leather, thigh boots weighed a man down too. The stacks behind him probably remain from last year's harvest in an area where several pits were dug simultaneously during the trade's heyday. Here, in the 1920s not far from Reach, the diggers were never young. This man's trade might just last him to the end of his working life but the young already saw it as an anachronism.

(Cambridgeshire Collection)

DRY CONDITIONS

The season coming to an end and comfortable in the pit, but make no mistake, this man would not have been digging turf if it had been as dry as it appears here. All turf had to come out wet, otherwise it would have crumbed in the handling and never shrunk hard for burning. Dried turves were handled several times and should lose nothing in the process. After all, they were used as bricks in ancient times. This digger would find water in his trench next morning. With Reach lodebank in the distance, the stacks have built up again. This is the 1920s, the diggers few and far between but productive.

(Cambridgeshire Collection; Reid)

DRESSING

Once more the dressing, or opening, of the turves, here clearly demonstrated, re-stacking the turves criss-cross. From the eighteen by four-and-a-half inches becket the turves would shrink to about eleven by three-and-a-half inches before hardening. Generally the dug turves could be handled three weeks after the digging as facilitated here, but this always depended on the weather. Speed may have been essential to the digger but he was never rushed. The drying brought a considerable weight loss in the turves and strong winds could sometimes blow the dressed rows over. We are still in Swaffham Fen in the 1920s.

(Cambridgeshire Collection)

STACKING

When such huge stacks as these were left on the fen all winter and into spring they were sometimes found to be hosts to wrens, their nests made secure with food enough at hand - and water, needless to say. As they dried the turves exposed their contents - sometimes all too readily, meaning they had been dug a little too near the surface and contained elements that flared. The locals called them 'pipey' turves full of 'reed torts' and would readily complain. Smouldering was essential to their effectiveness, but all men are fallible, all sometimes a little careless against their better judgement. The man is building a 'hand' at a time, the way that does it best. The industry had but a decade to go.

(Cambridgeshire Collection)

FROM THE PIT

This is August 1930 in Swaffham Fen where the digger saves bending by dressing his turves from the pit. These bogs, and those between Burwell and Wicken had been dug from the twelfth century and there were still rich seams of peat as this worker saw his trade into its last decade. There is indeed plenty left today for the farmers although the surface is eroding down all the time - something like two inches a year. One day the surface will be clay - or under water - the substance of farming there as well as the old turf trade, a fading memory.

(Cambridgeshire Collection; Hatfield)

LOADING THE CART

The digger soon recognized the quality of the turf he had uncovered. If it was poor he might have to dig lower down, but the decision was the boss's. Both were like farmers knowing the quality of their soil, but poor turves did find their way onto the market. It is August 1930 in Swaffham Fen and relatively firm underfoot. Reach Lode is nearby but transporting all the way by pony and cart is safe and therefore faster. When the demand was greatest the land route to these stacks would be treacherous so now was the time to lay in store in the villages. All the droves in Swaffham Fen giving access to farmland as well as these turf pits were mires in winter and it was not until 1941 that concrete surfaces were laid to facilitate the moving of crops for the war effort. The hawker is happy in his work in such weather in spite of the onlooker.

(Cambridgeshire Collection; Hatfield)

A BOATLOAD

The surest means of transport in all seasons stays moored on Reach Lode in the 1920s, a time when its destination would be Burwell or Reach sooner than Upware. The turf trade from the towns had about ceased and only local consumption kept the trade alive. Upware, nevertheless would want its own supply, much of it fetched by drove. Bert Bailey claimed that the last turf he dug in Swaffham Fen was the best he had ever seen. Having taken all those years to find it, it must have felt like a cruel rebuttal.

(Cambridgeshire Collection)

A DEMONSTRATION

In 1961, twenty-two years after hanging up his becket, Bert Bailey takes it down
to give a demonstration of his old trade to a journalist and his photographer. He
would have expected to be paid for it and not only with beer. He was interviewed
many times and with difficulty only when in his nineties when deafness afflicted
him. He was willing then but lost his way with pronunciation.

SENNITT'S PITS

In the 1970s by the derelict farm where he was born beside Burwell Lode Harold Sennitt dug turf pits as an attraction for visitors. He never entered the trade but was a farmer wanting to find out for himself how turf digging was done. Then the visitors came, followed by television cameras and a film of him working. He gathered together a collection of turf tools, some having survived alternative uses in the meantime. Farmers had taken to using the old beckets to chop up mangolds and the moor spades found many uses in the muddy fens.

(Author's Collection)